JOANNA MURRAY-SMITH

Joanna Murray-Smith's plays have been produced throughout
Australia and all over the world, including *Honour* which had
a public reading with Meryl Streep and was produced on
Broadway in 1998, and the National Theatre, London, in 2003.
Other plays include *Rapture, Nightfall, Redemption, Love
Child, Atlanta* and *Flame*, many of which have been translated
into other languages and adapted for radio. Her novels include
Truce (1994) and *Judgement Rock* (2002), both published by
Penguin Australia. She lives near Melbourne with her husband
and three children.

Joanna Murray-Smith

BOMBSHELLS

CURRENCY PRESS
Sydney
www.currency.com.au

NICK HERN BOOKS
London
www.nickhernbooks.co.uk

Bombshells was first published as a paperback original in 2004 jointly by Nick Hern Books Limited, 14 Larden Road, London W3 7ST, United Kingdom, and Currency Press Limited, PO Box 2287, Strawberry Hills, NSW 2012, Australia

Bombshells copyright © 2004 Joanna Murray-Smith

Joanna Murray-Smith has asserted her right to be identified as the author of this work

Cover photography: Caroline O'Connor in *Bombshells*. © Jeff Busby

Typeset by Country Setting, Kingsdown, Kent CT14 8ES, UK Printed and bound in the United Kingdom by Bookmarque, Croydon, Surrey

A CIP catalogue record for this book is available from the British Library

ISBN 1 85459 850 3 (UK)
ISBN 0 86819 751 3 (Australia)

Contents

BOMBSHELLS

Author's Note

Bombshells was originally conceived by Simon Phillips, the wonderfully cheerful and insightful artistic director of the Melbourne Theatre Company. Simon had long admired Caroline O'Connor and, at his suggestion, I wrote six characters to give full expression to Caroline's astonishing versatility as a performer.

'Women on the edge' was the uniting theme, and I found it disturbingly easy to apply my imagination to the madness which precipitates, inhabits or follows the point at which a woman's private and public selves intersect. It seemed to me that in the post-feminist era, women have forsaken one kind of madness with other kinds. Where once women went mad suppressing their ambitions or dreams, they now drive themselves mad trying to fulfil them all simultaneously, dissecting themselves under the microscope of self-analysis, disappearing inside the impossible pressures of the will to be good, to be great and to be true to every individual instinct. Many of us are trying to lead multiple lives: child, mother, wife, lover, star, giving small doses of oxygen to each and imploding under the weight of so many competing roles. The women I have written in *Bombshells* struggle sometimes hilariously, sometimes tragically, to bridge the chasm between the wilderness of their inner worlds and the demands of their outer worlds. And humour, in the end, is our saviour.

While *Bombshells* was inspired by Caroline, these characters belong to the wider world of female performance. I hope they will be performed from Vaduz to Vladivostok, by actresses of all ages, with a universal delight in the passionate, miserable, hilarious wildness of women.

My thanks go to director and friend Simon Phillips for telling me, for God's sake, to be *funny*, and for introducing me to the wonderful Ms O'Connor. Caroline and Simon first brought these words and women to life with great intelligence, endurance and panache, along with the brilliant creative endeavours of Elena Kats-Chernin, Shaun Gurton and David Murray. My thanks go to all of them and to the Melbourne Theatre Company for lighting the original fuse.

Joanna Murray-Smith

Bombshells was first presented by Melbourne Theatre Company at the Fairfax Theatre, Victorian Arts Centre, Melbourne, Australia, on 28 December 2001, with the following production team:

Perfomer   Caroline O'Connor
Director   Simon Phillips
Designer   Shaun Gurton
Composer   Elena Kats-Chernin
Lighting Designer   David Murray

This production was revived at the same venue from 26 February 2004 and transferred to the York Theatre, Seymour Centre, Sydney, Australia, from 30 April 2004.

A reduced version – consisting of four monologues – was presented as part of the Edinburgh Festival Fringe at the Assembly Rooms, Edinburgh, Scotland, from 6 August 2004. The performer again was Caroline O'Connor, directed by Simon Phillips.

This production – now consisting of all six monologues – transferred to the Arts Theatre, London, England, on 3 September 2004.

Four of the monologues from *Bombshells* were televised by the Australian Broadcasting Corporation in November 2003.

BOMBSHELLS

Characters

MERYL LOUISE DAVENPORT

TIGGY ENTWHISTLE

MARY O'DONNELL

THERESA McTERRY

WINSOME WEBSTER

ZOE STRUTHERS

Bombshells has been – and can be – adapted for each of the different countries where it is performed, making use of specific local references and place names. The Australian and British variations are incorporated in this published text, separated by a slash (/). For example, 'Paddle Pops / Mini Milks', '*Neighbours* / *EastEnders*' or 'Melbourne / London'.

MERYL LOUISE DAVENPORT

A thirty-something woman is on stage, alone. She begins very slowly and then builds in pace until she is on a frenetic stream-of-consciousness sprint.

MERYL. The baby cries. I open my eyes. It's darkish. The digital clock beside Barry says six-oh-seven. The baby needs a feed. The videos need to go back today. I need a coffee. I need to enquire about yoga. Gwyneth Paltrow does yoga. If I do yoga my life will begin to resemble Gwynnie's. Why does the baby need a feed? The baby down the road is sleeping through. *That* baby's a week younger than our baby. Is it the light? Is it the cold? Is it my diet? What are we doing wrong? I shouldn't have eaten the curry. I should have said no to the curry. I'm a selfish, hungry, greedy mother. What's wrong with our baby? Screaming. Screaming now.

Clomp, clomp, clomp. It's Amy. Amy gets into bed. Careful of the baby. I'm feeding the baby. Don't squash the baby. Amy's got a cold. Try to blow Amy's nose while feeding baby. How many countries are there in Africa? I don't know. You *should* know. I should know. I should know but I don't know. Switch breasts.

Ben's in the kitchen. I want Cocoslams. No. Yes. Cocoslams are evil. Cocoslams are not evil. Cocoslams are breakfast cereal. No, no, you can have Weetbix / Weetabix. Weetbix / Weetabix suck. You're not having Cocoslams. Psychopaths are evil. Child slavery is evil. Cocoslams are not evil. Liam's allowed to eat Cocoslams and how come everyone else gets a nice mother? Okay, eat the Cocoslams. Eat the damn Cocoslams! What's wrong with Ben? Ben doesn't like me and he's only eight. He already hates me. Why do I yell at him? Why can't I control myself? I've fucked up the last eight years and it's not his fault. He's the kid he's the kid I'm the mother I'm the mother – It's my fault because I'm an egomaniac and a control freak. How many countries are there in Africa? I don't know. How many do you *think* there are? I don't know, Amy. I'm trying to feed the baby. But how many do you *think* there are? Alright, thirty.

Baby in bassinet. Stick plug in baby's mouth. Get breakfast, quickly quickly, can't be late, always late, need a coffee, teacher said we have to make an effort to get Ben into class on time. Teacher said children suffer if they're late. Hurry hurry do the lunches hurry up, lunches, lunches –

Abandoning the idea.

– *money* for the lunches. Where's the money, where's the money, baby crying, in the shower, wash, quick, out, quick, dry, quick, clothes hurry hurry, Never look 'quite right', never look 'put together', never look 'well groomed'. Always dreamt I'd scoff at women who just threw themselves together. Now I am one. Lipstick, that'll do it, whack it on, that way the other mothers will think I'm in control, I'm on top of things. Where's the money for the leukemia-money-raising head-shaving of the Geography teacher? Where's the money for the children's hospital appeal? Amy needs the form signed for the excursion. Amy says it has to be in today. It *has* to be in today or I won't be allowed to go. It *has* to be, it *has* to be, it *has* to be. Need a coffee, need a coffee, keys keys keys KEYS. School bags tennis rackets handbag nappy-bag dry-cleaning dummy dummy school hats need hats keys keys keys KEYS.

In the car. Baby's got no socks. Need socks. Should go back in for socks. Can't be bothered. Selfish, awful mother. Baby has cold feet. Selfish, stupid, disorganised mother –

Brilliant idea dawning on her.

Pretend they fell off – babies are always losing socks.

There's the neighbour with her cacti, should be neighbourly, should chat, can't be bothered, sweet lady, all alone, husband dumped her, needs a nice neighbour, can't be bothered. Driving too fast. Truck. TrucktrucktrucktrucktruckTRUCK! *PRICK!!* Children's lives are more important than being punctual. But I *have* to be punctual. I *have* to be punctual or the teacher will think I'm a total failure. I *am* a total failure. I'm a failure and a fake and everyone can see through the lipstick. EVERYONE OUT!!

I know the truth about the socks. The baby's socks did not fall off. Amy's only on C books. Vanessa and Jamie and Alan are on R. Isabella and Georgia and Sandra are on N. Why is Amy on C? *What is wrong with Amy?* I don't read with her enough. I read magazines. I read magazines all the time, stupid, stupid expensive magazines about stupid celebrities. I care more about Renée Zellweger's favourite nail lacquer than about my own child. I'm the reason children can't read any more – I'm the reason literacy levels are down. I'm the reason children aren't equipped for life! It's my fault! I'm a lazy, selfish mother. Amy cries when I leave. I hug Amy. Teacher tells me to say goodbye and walk away. Amy sobs. Walk away. Want to go back and hug her but care more about what the teacher thinks of me than Amy's feelings.

Baby in car. Supermarket. Out of car. Other shoppers stare at sockless baby. Buy buy buy. Need detergent: Sunfresh, Lemonfresh, Freshmorning, Startfresh, Lemonsunfresh, Greendayfresh, Bubblemagic, Sparklefresh, Lemonsparkle, Morningfresh . . . Weetbix / Weetabix, Cornflakes, Special K, Ricebran, Branflakes, Oatmeal, Ricebubbles, Fruitloops, Muesli . . . Put Cocoslams in trolley. Toothpaste – probably gives you cancer, non-organic fruit, gives you cancer, Diet Pepsi, gives you cancer, salami makes the children obese, sweet biscuits, Paddle Pops / Mini Milks, white bread – cancer, I'm killing my children! I'm killing my children! None of the other mothers use white bread. I might as well line the kids up and shoot them, it would be quicker and more honest than poisoning them like this. *And cheaper.*

Home home gutters need doing house needs painting brothel brothel brothel BROTHEL Need a coffee. Baby crying, WHERE'S THE BABY?!

Washing, washing, baby lying on sheepskin, baby playing with stupid play mobile, needs proper interaction for development of brain and gross motor skills, babies need to be noticed not just plonked on sheepskins, baby growing up, these early days are so short, gone so fast, can't get them back, appreciate, appreciate, hurry up and appreciate, take the time, pull out the phone, lie down with baby –

Slowly.

– stare into baby's face –

Immediately faster.

No time for this! No time for this! Am I crazy? Washing, drying, phone ringing! Put baby to bed, need anti-depressants, got to have anti-depressants, can't take them, breast-feeding, need them, can't take them, want to feel happier but baby would be drugged now, get cancer later, can't do it, want to do it, selfish mother, wrong priorities. Vacuum, vacuum, don't move the furniture, can't be bothered, bad housekeeper, not even working, no excuse, need a coffee, need a coffee, proper coffee, got to pay the gas bill, promised I'd pay the gas bill, Barry's got enough to do, he's so nice to me, Barry's so nice to me, have to make things easier on him, look at me, look at me, I've let myself go, should go to the gym, should have some pride – need pride, *must* get it: castor sugar, chicken fillets, *pride*. Got to get Ben new karate uniform, got to get Amy Backstroke Barbie for birthday, got to organise party, got to make it a good party, got to be as good as Caitlyn's, Caitlyn's mother makes an effort, Amy thinks Caitlyn's mother is a superstar, *must* persuade her I am, got to get Backstroke Barbie, blonde or brunette, which does she want? Which does she want? Get *both*, then they can relay. Got to return Alex's call, got to call Allie, should visit Bernadette in hospital. Got to clean car – got to water the garden – fridge is filthy, need a coffee – need a coffee.

OKAY THAT'S IT. NEED A COFFEE!

Wake the baby, baby in car, selfish mother, selfish yuppie mother thinks her own caffe latte is more important than the baby's patterns, baby not in pattern, my fault, other babies have a pattern, other mothers don't wake their baby for a caffe latte, they have babies in patterns!

At the shops, got to pay the gas bill, pass newsagent, see new *Hello!* magazine, seven dollars / three pounds, should give it to leukemia shave-a-thon at school but need to know about obscure TV star's miracle baby – must have it, must have it, buy it, got to pay gas bill, pass gifty-ware shop, see useless aromatherapy candles, see sunglasses, got to have candles, fill the house with smell of roses, be houseproud, be a sensualist, pay attention to ambience, need sunglasses, need to look glamorous for Barry, need to look glamorous for the children, children need to respect me more, glasses will do it, *glasses make me look incredible*! Glasses make me look totally Nigella, *must* have them, *fuck the gas bill*! Need a coffee, got to have coffee, COFFEEEEEEEE!

Beat as she savours the coffee, then she starts up again.

Baby *still* no socks, pollution, rain starting, no pram-protector because I'm useless, 'Seven months, thank you, oh yes, doesn't sleep, naughty girl, up for adoption, sending her back, hoho, kicked off her socks' – I'm a horrible, lying, evil woman, lying to protect my own reputation! She thinks I'm a good mother! She thinks I know what I'm doing!

She's a poor deluded member of the public and I'm living a lie! Three o'clock. THREE O'CLOCK! Jesusjesusjesus-JESUS! Got to pick up the kids! Kids'll feel abandoned, kids'll be the only children in the schoolyard without a mother. Strap the baby in, strap twisted, should fix it, can't fix it, should fix it, fuck it, no time –

Hello children, beautiful children, yes, Caitlyn can play, everyone in, belts belts belts. Cyclist on left, silly cyclist, hate cyclists – cyclists should all be shot! EVERYONE OUT!!

Need to feed the baby, Amy and Caitlyn disappear, Ben says he hates school. Why does Ben hate school? Tell Ben I understand, it's okay, everyone hates school at some time in their school life, Ben says he HATES SCHOOL, I say I understand, baby cries, need to change the baby, disposables bad for environment, bad mother, Ben cries, NOT GOING TO SCHOOL ANY MORE, I say, now now, cheer up. NOT GOING, NOT GOING, NOT GOING! For God's sake, Ben, grow up, everyone has to go to school! School is not there to be enjoyed. School is something you just have to do. The Government will send Mummy to jail if you don't go. Ben crying: I don't want Mummy to go to jail! It's all right, I'm not going to go to jail! I DON'T WANT MUMMY TO GO TO JAIL! That was a stupid thing I said, Ben, the government doesn't put mothers in jail. THEN I'M NOT GOING TO SCHOOL.

Where are Amy and Caitlyn? Mustn't let anything happen to Caitlyn while she's my responsibility. Maybe Caitlyn and Amy are lying dead in the playroom, maybe they ate carpet cleaner, maybe they stuck bits of the Barbie jeep in the electric socket, they're pale and dead and electrocuted and I'm up here with *Hello!* magazine and a Kit Kat. Where's the baby? Where's the baby? WHERE'S THE BABY?

Looks down at breasts. With relief.

Switch breasts.

MENTAL NOTE: MUSN'T ACCIDENTALLY KILL
THE CHILDREN! Driving too fast, not looking, choking,
poisoning with food past used-by date, baby too hot, too
cold, not watched, mustn't sleep, mustn't sleep, mustn't
sleep, skateboards, bicycles, forget the helmet, not looking,
slack mother, slack mother, switch breasts, shopping malls,
children stolen, railway lines, drugs everywhere, I'm a mess,
they've got my genes, I'VE FUCKED THEM UP!! I've
fucked them up, it's all my fault, I'm good cop one day, bad
cop the next, I'm not mad enough to get help but I'm too mad
to be a good parent, I get angry, I don't get angry enough,
I'm inconsistent, I'm overbearing, I'm over emotional, I
care too much, I love too much, I'M TOO AFRAID!

How many countries are there in Africa? I know nothing,
I know nothing, if anyone knew how little I knew there'd be
an uprising, they'd take my kids away from me.

Baby's smiling – lovely baby – thinks I'm wonderful, not
for long, not for long, soon will realise. I just want to sit
with the baby. What would happen if I just got on a bus with
the baby, any bus, going somewhere, stay in a motel, just me
and the baby, I could sleep, I could sleep, I could sleep . . .

Phone ringing, fax going, videos videos, Amy – bath, Ben –
bath. Need a drink, becoming an alcoholic, only one drink,
but that's the way it starts – Forgot the dry-cleaning, didn't
pay the gas bill, there's Barry, kisses kisses – Dinner dinner,
news from work, someone's pregnant, someone's leaving,
someone's pissed off, tell him about my day, try to think of
something interesting – Can't think! Can't think! Nothing to
say! Used to be interesting! Used to be witty! Used to be
described as 'live wire'. It's all over. It's all over! Swallowed
up in sadness! Can't explain it! Barry would think I'm
crazy, Barry will give up on me! Run away with receptionist
with ankle bracelet – always happy – always laughing –
who could blame him? I'll be all alone! Can't fix fuses.

Can't understand phone-banking. Can't have sex with outside world, forgotten how. Life nearly over, nearly forty, face falling apart, want plastic surgery, too scary, too undignified, too expensive – *still* want plastic surgery – life half-over, don't want to die, don't want to leave children, don't want to be separate from Barry – if Barry dies I'm dying too, CAN'T LIVE WITHOUT BARRY – Who'll take the children, sister will take the children, sister's good mother, children will be okay – very sad – 'Father died, mother couldn't live without him' – sad story, have to deal with it, have to get over it, will eventually, good kids, smart kids, they'll be okay.

Kids in bed, kids want water, talk to Barry, kids want door open, yell at kids – Didn't water hydrangeas, didn't ring anyone, didn't get dry-cleaning, didn't pay gas bill – Didn't get to the gym – Didn't appropriately interact with baby, didn't handle conflict with Ben well – Didn't enquire about yoga – Didn't sort socks, didn't read the paper – Didn't sit around with other mothers, laughing convivially about motherhood. Didn't organise Amy's party. Didn't clean car. Didn't water garden. FUCKING VIDEOS! Feed baby, baby sleeping, kiss Barry. Dreaming, dreaming, darkness, stillness, silence . . .

Silence.

The baby cries. I open my eyes. It's darkish. Baby crying . . . Six-oh-seven . . .

TIGGY ENTWHISTLE

*A woman tentatively moves to a podium at the centre of the
stage. She reflects all the characteristics which she later uses
to describe the cacti: 'a covering of slender, soft hair . . .
slender, needle-like body . . . long, soft, woolly covering'.
She surveys the audience, appalled at the task before her.
Then musters her will and clears her throat. She is a picture
of timidity attempting to overcome itself. A slide projection
screen behind her is blank.*

TIGGY. Good afternoon.

She moves closer to the invisible microphone.

Good afternoon.

*It booms. Already deeply anxious, she moves halfway
back. Her tiny voice gradually builds in volume.*

Thank you –

Clears her throat.

Thank you for –

Clears throat, gathers courage.

– that very kind introduction, Kevin. My name is –

*She momentarily forgets, then in the nick of time recalls
it with relief.*

Tiggy Entwhistle –

Beat of relief.

– and it is my pleasure to be here tonight representing the North Heatherton Chapter of C.A.S.L.

Beat. With great deliberation, she pushes the slide remote-control and a slide of a group of ordinary folk, including her, stand in front of a large cactus. Surveying the audience:

I would like to start by saying that it is a privilege and a pleasure to be here.

More clearing of throat, gathering of courage.

Membership of this Society has provided me with a sense of belonging and the informal atmosphere of sharing information and pleasant interaction has meant much to me over the past personally trying twelve months. Those of you from North Heatherton know that I am a comparative newcomer to the world of succulents.

Slide of tall skinny cactus.

But I'm sure you'd agree – without wishing to blow my own trumpet at all – that I have made up for lost time with the dedication and passion I have applied to this remarkable plant. Toot! Toot!

Nervous laugh.

I don't think it's any secret to many of my North Heatherton cohort, that I have had an 'annus horribilis', to quote our admired patron.

Slide of Queen Elizabeth II.

And in the midst of my personal troubles, of which quite a few of you are aware, I can only stress that my cacti have played an essential part in holding me together.

I was not, in fact, going to make mention of this, but for Marjorie Venables – many of you know Marjorie – who took me aside when I was asked to speak today and said: 'Tiggy, if you want to do justice to our beloved friend the cactus, how better to show its significance than to tell the good people the way in which it has pulled you through the relentless pain of your existence.'

Beat.

Of course, many people might say:

'Why cacti?'

Beat.

Why cacti?

Beat.

Good question. Around the world and for centuries, people have been asking just what it is about the succulents that draws people in. These plants have many useful applications. Over the centuries, varieties of succulents have found practical use as food and medicine –

Abstract, pointless slide of food and medicine.

– and primitive societies even used their fibres for the construction of rope, bedding and clothes –

Another pointless slide of a mattress.

But the usefulness of the cacti is only half the story! They are a life-affirming ingredient in the melting pot of environmental splendour! We regard the cactus as a plant which struggles to survive in a hostile environment, and it is this notion of proud, undaunted struggle, which enhances its appeal. It refuses to give in. It simply refuses to bow to circumstance, and it is this resoluteness, which makes many of us proud to say: I LOVE CACTI.

Beat. With quiet certainty:

And I don't believe it is too far-fetched to say that my cacti love me. When Harry . . . when all that happened . . . I could feel the companionship of the cacti flooding over me.

There are very few cactophiles who do not see their succulents as members of a valued extended family. The cactus is not, for instance, like a rose. It is not like a begonia or a daisy, lovely as they are.

Slide of a rose with a brutal 'X' across it.

The most endearing aspect of the cactus is the deceptiveness of its attraction. And this is where it is important to counteract the many myths about cacti. Despite popular belief, their spines are not poisonous, and the common assumption that they flower only once every seven years is completely untrue. *I can flower again and again and again.* He didn't believe me, he didn't think we could recapture . . . but the point is, he wouldn't even . . .

Composing herself:

During the cooler months or on days of full sun, a fine mist of water will help to avoid the unpleasant shrivelling of mature plants. Do you see? Do you see? A fine mist is all it takes. Is that too much to ask? Is it? IS IT? Harry, is that too much to ask? A mist of – of sweetness – of – love – a faint spray of compassion or – or fantasy – something – something. We're not talking about fancy-schmansy orchids here or big bossy show-offy lilies –

In quick succession, slide of lilies with brutal 'X' through them, slide of TIGGY and Harry at a dance in a church hall staring at the camera, slide of camellias with brutal 'X' through them.

– or passive aggressive camellias – not at all! It's not like they whine! It's not like they sit there on the windowsill saying: 'Please! Please! Look at me! Think of me! Touch me! Flatter me! LOVE me!' No. No. They sit quietly. They watch game-shows and crochet and bake and occasionally tidy up and try to show a degree of compassion and affection to those around them and keep themselves nice with exercise videos and occasionally talk to friends on the phone and read the odd romance novel. That's what they do! That's what they do! *And it's too much, it's too much to honour that?* To honour that? To feel something – anything – for that?

Beat.

It's not like I don't do anything! I cared for you! And all the time . . . all the time . . . you were planning an escape – you and – oh, don't pretend! Don't pretend! I've seen her with her midriff and her pierced belly button! We've all seen her. Young Mary O'Donnell was putting up posters for the school talent show outside Harvester and told her mother Elspeth O'Donnell who told Vera McTerry who told Marjorie Venables at book club who told me – that you and some flibbertigibbet were looking very cosy over the salad bar. And what do you suppose is going to happen when she comes to see the real you, Harry? – Not the Harry that pays for the Chinese –

Slide of crumbled fortune cookie and bill.

– I found the bill with a fortune cookie all crumbled up in your sports jacket: 'A wise man seizes the moment' – When she sees the Harry who falls asleep at eight p.m., the Harry that gets a rash at any public event, the Harry with tinea! As if a fat, balding, forty-nine-year-old, lactose-intolerant, fare-infringement officer is going to set *anyone* on fire. You and your big dreams! You're going to come completely UNSTUCK AND YOU'RE GOING TO DIE ALONE, UNDISCOVERED FOR WEEKS –

Beat.

– IN A CARAVAN.

Long beat. New slide of two forlorn cacti: the original skinny, straight one and a squat round one standing side by side.

At the commencement of the nineteenth century, private
collectors competed for rare breeds and possessed many of
the largest collections in Europe. But after some time,
succulents were no longer fashionable. The fascination with
these plants diminished. The fascination . . . diminished . . .
Okay, it diminished. All right. Okay. Fair enough. But it's
not like anything stays the same! No one expects it to be
like it was at the start, for ever! It starts as passion, it starts
with something dangerous, and then the danger starts to
fade and something else – something else takes its place . . .
something tender and fine and hardy, something ancient and
resonant and sweet . . . And all the headiness, the deep,
dizzy enchantment becomes something of a higher order
and that's when – *that's* when people become lovers,
become *true lovers* . . . when their feet touch the ground
and they know they've brought something of the madness
back to earth.

   Quietly and building:

I always knew I was lucky to have you – felt as if the fact
you wanted me taught me I was better than I imagined. Your
glance made me feel lovely! Your hands on my skin made
me feel . . . lit . . . lit from within, like a lamp switching
on . . . And in the midst of a world gone to pieces . . . with
planes in towers and suicide bombers, and ordinary acts
of plain unkindness and selfishness and unfriendliness and
sadness and misery and loss all around, there we were.
There we were. A core. A tiny beating heart of ordinary
happiness. And goodwill. And . . . hope. Hope.

   Beat.

Harry! Harry! Harry! COME BACK!

   Long beat.

Great care must be used when the decision is made to
replant a cactus. Consideration must be paid to the existing
ball of roots, and damage avoided at all costs. That said,

dead or diseased roots should be *hacked off with a sharp instrument!* This will – The thing is, that this will – furnish – It will furnish the cactus with a chance to . . . It will furnish the cactus with a very real chance to . . .

MARY O'DONNELL

*A teenage schoolgirl on stage. As she speaks, she
commences dressing in an amateurish 'cat' costume.*

MARY. *No one* can sing and dance like me. No one in the
whole school. I am the Liza Minnelli of St Brigid's and
nobody can say I'm not. I've got a better voice than Angela
McTerry. Much better. Her only claim to fame is that she
has breasts bigger than her head, of which I am envious . . .
not. And I can dance which Angela McTerry cannot do even
though she thinks she can. She has not got the physique.
Angela McTerry does not look attractive in a leotard and
somebody who loves her should tell her so. She's got calves
the size of the Soviet Union just like her sister Theresa
McTerry – who's getting married to Ted 'The Pot-plant'
Swinbank on Saturday and thereby introducing the world to
the lovely vision of Angela in tangerine chiffon. And she's
got tickets on herself just because her father's on *Neighbours /
EastEnders*. Like *Neighbours / EastEnders* is a big deal.
Neighbours / EastEnders is *not* a big deal. The talent show
is a big deal. I love the talent show. *I love the talent show*.
So far there's no one who even comes close. Allison
Stoddard's one-woman *Waiting for Godot* was a wank.
Janice McElhone's 'Islands in the Stream' didn't cut it –
someone should have told her it's a duet. Veronica
O'Grady's 'Abba Medley' was a travesty. *A travesty*. I hope
Björn and Benny never hear about it. Veronica O'Grady
would be banned from Sweden.

Mr Burbridge said: 'Mary O'Donnell, the talent show is
coming up so you had better get thinking, young lady.' Mr

Burbridge knows that I *am* the talent show. The talent show
would be nothing without me. It would be 'the *show*'. The
show. Because I *am* the talent. Okay. Okay. Here we go.
This is your last rehearsal, Mary O'Donnell. Do not stuff
it up. Do not stuff it up.

*Lights up. Music on. She rips into the final two minutes
of 'O'Shaunnesy', a showtune not unlike 'Macavity the
Mystery Cat' from* Cats, *complete with brilliantly executed
choreography incorporating every cliché known to
musical theatre.*

O'Shaunnesy's a whiskery cat:
He's called the crooked claw,
For he's the fearless feline
Who has wicked things in store.
The frazzlement of Interpol,
With savage savoir faire,
He's the cat who never takes the rap,
With his evil pussy stare.
O'Shaunnesy, O'Shaunnesy,
There's no one like O'Shaunnesy,
He's a cunning little kitty of devilish dishonesty.
He'll prowl your yard and make a mess,
He'll be up for any dare.
Whenever there's catastrophe,
O'Shaunnesy, O'Shaunnesy, O'Shaunnesy, O'Shaunnesy –

Music.

Whenever there's catastrophe,
O'Shaunnesy's been there!

Okay, okay, you're ready. You're ready, and baby, you are
going to knock their socks off! *No one* can give a song what
I can give it. Not Veronica O'Grady. Not Sally-Anne
O'Malley. Not Angela McTerry.

ANNOUNCER. And now we have Angela McTerry
performing that timeless number: 'O'Shaunnesy, the

Mystery Cat'.

MARY (*quietly*). *What did he say?*

   Beat.

What did he say? 'O'Shaunnesy'? 'O' Fucking Shaunnesy'?
Angela McTerry has stolen my number! No. No. It's not
possible. It's not possible. IT IS NOT GOING TO HAPPEN.

   The music starts. MARY *turns to watch from the wings*
   as the invisible Angela McTerry performs 'O'Shaunnesy'.
   The music is in the background as we hear MARY*'s*
   thoughts.

Oh great. Oh fabulous. Angela McTerry is doing my party
piece and I am left with precisely . . . nothing. Nothing. I've
been rehearsing this fucking number for weeks. And now
what? Am I going to let Angela McTerry steal *my* thunder?
Am I going to let Angela McTerry win the talent show?
Am I going to let Angela McTerry have her ugly face on the
front of the *St Brigid's Bugle*? Am I going to be pipped at
the post by Angela McTerry? NO, I AM NOT.

Okay. Okay. Stay calm. Stay calm. You'll think of
something. This is actually very useful. Very useful. Just
like showbiz. Things happen. Plans come unstuck but the
SHOW MUST GO ON. This is the point at which a true
artiste just pulls something astonishing right out of the bag.
I can do it. I can do it. I'm Mary O'Donnell, the woman
who put the 'razzle dazzle' into St Brigid's!

   Beat.

I'll improvise. That's what real performers do. That's what
Al Pacino does! That's what's Meryl Streep does! She just
makes it up. She lets the spirit of her profound creativity
run free. I'll dance like no one's danced before!

   Rushing to her CD collection.

Look at the CDs. What CDs did I bring . . . ? Pointer Sisters

. . . Falco . . . Carpenters . . . Shaft.

Beat.

SHAFT.

Beat.

Shaft.

Beat. Slowly building:

'Mary O'Donnell performs a dance routine from that classic of soul and groove: Shaft!' 'Mary O'Donnell does Shaft!' 'What did Mary O'Donnell do?' 'SHE DID SHAFT.' Who else has danced to Shaft? Who else at St Brigid's has communed with that big black mother Isaac Hayes? Nobody, that's who! Could Angela McTerry do Shaft? No, she could not! I could do 'O'Shaunnesy' but she could not do Shaft! I can do Isaac Hayes! I can be soulful! I can be groovy! I CAN BE BLACK! After all, the similiarities are spooky: the performer is a Catholic schoolgirl and the song is about a –

A touch of doubt as she reads the CD cover notes:

– Super-Hip Renegade African-American Cop . . . He walks the mean streets of Hell's Kitchen and she walks the mean streets of . . . St Brigid's. He's trying to subvert the mainstream dialectic for the benefit of his black brothers in Harlem and she's trying to subvert the mainstream dialectic for her white sisters in Lower Templestowe / Lower Sydenham. I can be anyone I want to be! I've got style! I've got pizazz! I've got . . . thirty-four seconds to come up with something!

ANNOUNCER. Thank you Angela! And what a super rendition of that magical number it was. And now we have Mary O'Donnell, who won last year's talent show with that extraordinary version of 'My Heart Will Go On'. This year, Mary brings us a dance interpretation of –

Longish beat.

Shaft.

> MARY *gingerly makes her way onto centre stage and peers out at the audience. She gets into position. The music begins. From this point on, Mary has to invent the choreography, trying to keep physically in sync with the song's rhythm and instrumental 'moments'.*

MARY. Jesus Jesus Jesus Jesus Jesus, HELP ME! This is Mary O'Donnell speaking, God. I go to St Brigid's. I am enormously ENORMOUSLY talented, oh God, and it would be a travesty if Angela McTerry won the talent show. I know this may not sound very important to you, God, but I'm telling you that if Angela McTerry wins, it is not simply a win for the McTerry family including Theresa, a trollop *par excellence*, but a win for Satan himself. Because Angela McTerry *is* Satan, God. Believe me, I know. I'm telling you that if Angela McTerry wins then you have LOST THE RACE AND HUMANITY IS DOOMED. I have prayed to you every day of my life and now, NOW is the moment I am calling in a favour from you. Can you hear me, God? Please. If you can hear me, make the music jump now.

> *The compact disc jumps.*

Okay, okay. He's on my side. I can do this! I can do this!

> MARY *attempts a daring leg-split which works perfectly in time with the musical moment. Her confidence soars.*

'Who's the Black Private Dick; Who's the Sex Machine to all the Chicks?' I am! Mary O'Donnell is that sex machine. 'Who's the cat who won't cop out when there's danger all about?' I am! I am the Bad Mother of St Brigid's and you had better watch out for me!

> *Physical hilarity as* MARY, *lip-syching the original track, improvises a brilliant, sexually-charged routine in imitation of the Shaft character, and then, increasingly*

exhausted, desperately incorporates moments from the
'O'Shaunnesy' performance, Irish dancing, etc. Finally
the song comes to an end and the totally worn-out
MARY *brings her dance to a close. The audience erupts.*
MARY *laps up the applause, then waits on tenterhooks,*
her face a picture of nervous anticipation.

ANNOUNCER. Thank you, Mary. Ladies and gentlemen,
boys and girls, the winner of the St Brigid's Talent Show
is –

THERESA McTERRY

A bride in her white fancy underwear on stage.

THERESA. Delirious!

Beat.

I am so fucking happy! I'm so happy I could scream.

She screams.

I look incredible. I look like a . . . like a fairytale –

She checks out her suspenders, etc.

Hooker. /

Beat.

Regard as the bride slips on her slip. Slipping on her slip . . . The silk slip glides over her well-defined torso . . . buffed and polished like a – like a –

Struggling:

– buffed and polished thing. Reflect a moment on the bride. She stands on the cusp between the world of dreams and the world of fulfilment, of girl to woman, of me-ness to us-ness . . .

Pausing to appreciate her words:

LOVELY!

She regards herself in the mirror.

I am so fucking, fucking happy! I've been waiting for this day since third form when Leanne Snowball and I planned

our Big Days whilst tanning our legs outside the maths
room. At that point I was very much into the Bianca-Jagger-
white-tuxedo look, seventies Eurotrash-Amalfi-Coast-
private-jet kind of thing. I imagined my married life in a
Knightsbridge town house with a bunch of Afghans . . . as
in the dogs not the refugees. Afghans were very much the
'in-dog' for a while. But in the seventies, anyone who was
anyone looked like an Afghan . . . Veruschka, Marisa
Berenson, David Bowie . . . Leanne wanted a wedding dress
with big fur cuffs and a muff . . . a muff being a kind of
unattached pocket you stuck your hands in . . . Very Marie-
Osmond-Winter-Wedding-in-Salt-Lake-City kind of thing . . .
Although life being what it is, Leanne actually got married
in a wetsuit at Sea World . . . Anyhoo, I've got Ted. Ted.
What a guy. What a lucky girl. What a lucky, lucky . . . *Ted.*
And who wouldn't love Ted?

Beat.

In an hour I'm going to be somebody's wife! *I'm going to
be somebody's wife. Somebody. Anybody. A wife. A wifely
wife. A wifey wife. A Wife. Wife.* WIFE . . . Weird word.
'Wife.' I've never really thought about it before. It sounds
like . . . a kitchen implement.

Bellows:

'HAS ANYBODY SEEN THE WIFE?'

Bellows back:

'IT'S IN THE DISHWASHER!'

Beat.

The point is, I'm going to *belong* to someone! I'm not
going to be floating on that endless ocean of singlehood.
Ted has thrown me a lifebuoy and I'm taking it! Ted has
rescued me from eternal nights with girlfriends complaining
about men, leg-waxing, *Cosmopolitan*-reading, Lean-

Cuisine-eating, wardrobe-obsessing desperation! No more
pounding tick of the biological clock.

Building in volume from tiny whisper to yell:

Tickticktickticktick**TICKTICKTICK***TICKTICK TICK!!*

*She picks up an imaginary mallet and smashes the clock,
then basks in the silence.*

Ted and I are linked by a love that will endure, built on lust
and youth, fed on time, nurtured on struggle and achievement,
grown through babies, anniversaries, promotions, sustained
through illness, tragedy and loss, a deep, driving, delicate,
idiosyncratic, sweet-natured, forgiving, complex kind of
love, *a love for life* . . . We're going to be one of those
couples who go out to dinner and say nothing at all. Not
because we have nothing to say to each other, not because
we're bored to death, not because everything that could be
said has been said, not because we're tired from organising
the kids – getting the babysitter – tired before we even go
out, not because we've realised that when all is said and
done we just don't have anything in common, not because
we've finally cottoned on to the fact that lust is not the same
as like and now that lust has gone . . . we just annoy each
other – No! *NO!* But because *words cannot do justice to the
immensity of our emotions* . . . we sip, we sup, we lick, we
chew, we go home and reflect that love lifts us up . . .

Trying to think of something to finish with.

Where we belong . . .

She slips on her dress and regards herself in the mirror.

The beautiful bride was wearing a superb full-length silk
satin gown with beaded bodice and sweetheart neckline,
accessorised by cream satin slingbacks, traditional veil, a
simple posy of lily of the valley and a heartfelt intention to
prove the statistics wrong.

Beat.

You know, this is the happiest day of my life. Truly, the happiest. I'm so ready to make the announcement to the world that two young people love each other enough to forsake the path of perpetual self-gratification.

She puts on her veil and regards herself.

Princess! Princess Grace, Princess Diana, Audrey Hepburn, Posh Spice, Jennifer Aniston, Jennifer Lopez. Me. Me. Me.

She takes a deep breath, opens the door and walks out into the congregation. The music begins and she starts to walk.

THERE HE IS, THERE HE IS, THERE HE IS, OH MY GOD OH MY GOD MY GOD MY GOD MY GOD, IT'S HAPPENING! IT'S REALLY HAPPENING! I *want* to be possessed. I want to be held, nurtured, nestled, owned. I want to lie around in negligees eating cream buns. I want to roam the high plains of the domestic interior barefoot and pregnant, moving languidly between kitchen and bedroom, nourishing the varied appetites of the man I love. I want to be a golden, glowing orb of femininity, I want to excel at supporting and obeying . . . I want to be Pammy Anderson meets Laura Bush . . . I do love Ted. I said that, didn't I? You do love Ted, don't you, Theresa? Yes, I do.

She reaches the imaginary groom. She lifts the veil back.

Hello Ted! Hello, every morning and every night for the rest of my life! Hello, man of my dreams!

Sweetly:

Ted.

She takes him in, this time with a little less conviction:

Ted.

Now really not sure at all:

Ted Ted Ted Ted. What's with the mauve cummerbund? He looks like the waiter from the Love Boat. And he's so short. He looks like . . . a pot plant . . . I can barely see him . . . He makes the vicar look like Schwarzenegger . . . And he shouldn't have gotten Trent to be best man – he's too tall. Trent.

A knowing smile.

Easter before last. Got me to stand on the Yellow Pages in spiked heels up against the dining room wall . . . Ted would never get me to stand on the Yellow Pages, Ted's a flat-on-your-back kind of a fellow and that's fine, that's fine, each to his own, and for a lifetime situation, you're probably not going to want to stand on the Yellow Pages in a pair of stilettos.

Listen, if it doesn't work out, life goes on. We've got the apartment. House prices are going through the roof. If we don't divorce for five years, we'll have paid it off and Ted's got the investment property – that's got to be worth something. His dad's shares – there's probably ten thousand or so in those.

Warming to the thought:

So hang on, hang on, the apartment's probably worth two fifty, two fifty plus Ted's flat, that's got to be a hundred and eighty by now, it's only one bedroom but that area is going through the roof, maybe it's two by now, say it's two twenty, no, okay, be conservative, say it's one eighty, so two fifty and one eighty is . . . okay, there's four thirty and let's not even talk about the shares, so I could walk away tomorrow with two fifteen –

Beat. With renewed zeal:

Here we go. Here we go. What's Ted saying? What's Ted saying? *We should never have written our own vows!*

'I promise to nurture you like a small sapling growing beside the mighty river of love. I promise to water you and dispense sunlight over you and allow you to grow into a –

Beat. Trying to get her mouth around it:

Large. Sturdy. Trunk.' – The vicar looks kind of sexy in that outfit – 'I promise to grow beside you and protect you from the elements of life and to provide companionship to you as we become part of the forest of togetherness.'

Back to interior reality:

Do vicars have sex? In just a couple of seconds I will never be able to have sex with this vicar or any other living man. *Or dead.* Living or dead. They're all totally off the cards. They're gone, they're over, they're not even a blip on the radar. From now on it's me and the girls down one end of the table talking about George Clooney, and Ted and the boys down the other talking about stock options. Do you love Ted, Theresa? Do you regret it? Do you regret it? Do you regret it?

Beat.

I do.

Beat. Quietly:

What have I done?

Beat. Quietly:

What have I done?

Beat.

I only really wanted to wear the dress. The dress. The dress. It's all about the dress.

Beat. Building in volume and speed:

Outside the maths room. Me and Leanne Snowball talking about the dress the dress the dress. When Ted asked, when he turned to me, straight away I thought, I thought: The dress! The dress! And telling Mum. Mum cried. She put her hands flat on on her cheeks. Mum yelled: The dress! When I told the girls – I told the girls – they cried. The dress! The dress! It's all about the dress! Plunging neckline, high neck, sweetheart, strapless, slim-fitting, loose-fitting, layered, netted, textured, embroidered, beaded, cream, white, ivory, gold, glacial, elegant, striking, imaginative, a triumph, a triumph, a triumph! *It's all about the dress!*

'You may – ?' 'You may – ?' What's he – ? What's he – ? 'You may kiss' – 'You may kiss' . . .

Dawning on her:

The bride.

IT'S THE DRESS'S FAULT. The dress is to blame. The dress is to blame. I'M SUING THE DRESS!

Beat. Change of lighting to indicate we are at the reception. THERESA *starts dancing, backwards, with an imaginary Ted, the ubiquitous appalling dancer. She sings along with rapturous innocence, punctuated by her screams for help:*

WHAT THE FUCK HAVE I DONE?

. . .

'WATCH THE SLINGBACKS, TED, THEY COST FOUR HUNDRED SMACKEROOS.'

. . .

Oh my God, oh my God, oh my God. IT'S TOO LATE. IT'S OVER. IN A MINUTE THERE'LL BE SPEECHES AND THE CAKE AND THEN EVERYBODY GOES AWAY AND WE'RE ALL BY OURSELVES!

*Somebody cuts in and she is whisked in the other
direction.*

I'm going to be alone with Ted – and not just for the
weekend. Oh no. No. Not the weekend. A fraction longer
than the weekend. A *lifetime*. Ted and me, me and Ted, me
and Ted and – it gets worse! It gets worse! Me and Ted and
Ted's mother! Ted's mother, who thought Porcini Risotto
was an Italian sculptor! Ted's mother who wore cream lace
to her son's wedding like *SHE* DOESN'T HAVE ANY
MAJOR PSYCHOLOGICAL PROBLEMS. Look at the
bridesmaids! Look at them! 'Hi Kelly! Hi Nicole! Hi
Britney! You all look gorgeous!'

Jesus Christ, those bridesmaids' dresses are hideous! I had
four dried apricots following me up the aisle!

*Her father cuts in and whisks her back in the other
direction.*

'Hello Dad! Don't be sad, Dad! Don't be sad! Not lost a
daughter, gained a . . . pot plant!' What am I saying? What
am I saying? I should be happy! I should be radiantly,
radiantly happy! Ted stood on the deck and looked out at all
the drowning single girls with their smudged mascara and
their high-heels, bobbing in the waves of inarticulate
despair, waving desperately, and he threw me a line – and
then he hauled me up and over the side onto the HMS
Security, dutifully captained by fear, crewed by loneliness,
self-loathing and physical disintegration –

*Slowing down as she takes the impact of what she's
saying:*

– sailing upon the Ocean of Wedlock towards the well-
known ports of –

Beat. Slowly:

– boredom, resignation and regret . . .

Look! Look over there! Marjorie and Helen and Winsome whatsername – wandering through life with Fletcher Jones / BHS accounts and gallery membership, husbands all perfectly perfectly *dead*. I only have to wait . . . twenty, thirty years!

Urgently:

'Mum! MUM! . . . '

She spots her mother through the crowd, grabs her and hustles her to one side in a huddle. As she speaks, she becomes increasingly panicked, building in pitch:

Mum, Mum! You were right! You were right! I was wrong! I admit it! I admit it! You were totally totally completely right! . . . About Ted, Mum. You're totally right. HE'S NOT GOOD ENOUGH FOR ME. HE'S COMPLETELY WRONG. HE'S THE WRONG MAN. HE'S NOT THE ONE. HE IS NOT THE ONE, MUM. IT'S ALL A DREADFUL MIX-UP. Do you remember when I bought the orange culottes because I got carried away in the moment and wanted to be the kind of person who suited orange culottes, and you made me take them back? Well, Ted *is* the orange culottes.

Whispering:

Now very quietly, very quietly, without drawing attention to ourselves, I want you to take me home and put me to bed with a hot-water bottle and a cocoa. Now.

Loud:

NOW . . .

Her attention is distracted. She looks to an imaginary focus, smiles artificially and raises her glass to an imaginary toast.

Thank you for those kind words, Trent . . . I don't think so . . . Oh no, no, I don't think so . . . Really? A few words?

She moves to an imaginary microphone, her step leaden.
She pauses, takes in the audience.

Guests –

And takes a deep, slow breath and says quietly,
defeatedly:

I am so fucking happy. I am so happy I could scream.

She opens her mouth to scream.

WINSOME WEBSTER

An older, nicely dressed, conservative-looking woman on stage.

WINSOME. On Mondays, I go to the pictures with the widows. On Mondays, it's cheaper for senior citizens, so we just see whatever's on and afterwards we have a toasted sandwich and a coffee. On Tuesdays, I go walking with the widows. The beach, the dogs, whatever. On Wednesdays, I play bridge with the widows. Thursdays, we have book club. On Fridays, I do volunteer work for the Blind Society, and in the evening, the widows and I have dinner at that little place on the Boulevard. You know that one – it has the famous Salad Niçoise that everyone carries on about. They have the Widows' Special: two courses for twenty-five dollars / nine ninety-nine, including a glass of Riesling and coffee. Sometimes on a Saturday evening, I'll have dinner with one of the widows, at her place or mine. And on Sundays, generally speaking, I'll talk to a widow or two on the telephone.

Beat.

My husband, Jim, died ten years ago from cancer. Helen's husband, also Jim, died eight years ago from cancer. Marilyn's husband, Ken, died thirteen years ago from cancer. Allison's husband, Ben, died four years ago from cancer. And Vonnie's husband, Alan, died last year. Heart.

Beat.

In our society, being alone can make one feel rather silly. We sit there by ourselves, resolutely getting on with life, but feeling the awkwardness of being unlucky. Being unlucky is terribly unglamorous. There is nothing like pity to make you feel dull. It's hard to understand how *sympathy* has the reputation of being a nice thing to offer another person, when really it cuts like a knife.

   Beat.

One insulates oneself from the foolishness of being one by creating inordinate amounts of ritual, appearing as if every day is filled with significant pursuits with significant others. The irony is that what you long for, what you fantasise about when you're a widow, is the unexpected. The totally unexpected. Because while you know that anything *can* happen to a widow, anything *doesn't.*

There's something about being widowed. You can really only confide in other widows. Sisters don't get it. Married friends don't get it. Daughters don't get it. It's a different kind of loneliness. When you're two, it doesn't take all that long before you forget you were ever one. Then suddenly . . . suddenly . . .

I was thinking the other day that some enterprising . . . widow . . . should start a business which simply offers the service of decision-making. You ring them up and say, I can't decide whether to go with the more expensive hot-water service that promises this-that-the-other or the cheaper one which looks perfectly fine, and they tell you. Or you say: 'Should I get the couch recovered in a corduroy or a velvet?' They do the husband-job minus the personality. They don't say things like 'For God's sake, Winsome, you're not still banging on about that couch.' They say: 'Velvet, because it's timeless.' I would pay for that service, and so would the other widows, except for Marilyn who is pathologically mean. Marilyn went on a backpacking holiday to Vietnam. At seventy-eight. And it's not as if she can't afford to do it decently – she's more than comfortable. When we saw Zoe Struthers at Mural Hall / Fairfield Hall –

she was out here and, really, they don't make singers like
that any more – Marilyn spent seventy dollars / forty
pounds on a ticket but baulked at paying five dollars / three
pounds for a Chardonnay, I ask you. Anyway, decisions are
what kill us.

So what are one's weapons when one is a widow? Money?
Money helps. We all started to read the business pages
when the husbands died, learning to read the language of
the stock market the way we had once read recipes. Money.
And wit.

Wit, perhaps, is the only real weapon for survival. It fights
off melancholy, frightens sentimentality and gives the floral
shirt-maker, navy blue court-shoe image of the widow a bit
of an 'edge'. It gives us the silent upper hand when our
daughters patronise us . . .

It was a Friday in May when I got the call. It was the lady
from the Society saying that I had a new client. A young
blind student, male, doing his arts degree, lived independently
in a house, needed a reader. Fine, I said. To be honest, I was
tired of reading for Mrs Delahunt, since the only author she
liked was Anita Brookner. I used to say: 'Mrs Delahunt,
would you like me to read you some Tom Clancy?' And
she'd say, 'No, Winsome, if you don't mind, I'd like that
Anita Brookner again. The depressing one about the
widow.' Frankly, I could have just given Mrs Delahunt a
run-down of my week and it would have been indistinguish-
able from the new Anita Brookner bestseller. However, it is
one of the clear rules of the Society that readers do not
impose their views on the client. It's not my place. I'm there
to be their eyes, not their taste or their conscience.

I used to take scones with me to Mrs Delahunt's and we'd
have tea in between the first half hour and the second, to
give my voice a break. But with the new client, I thought,
well, being a young man, he might not be the scone type,
so I didn't take anything.

Beat.

I got the train to town and then took the bus almost to his door. He lived in one of those inner-city neighbourhoods near the university. It was a Victorian terrace, nice little front garden with David Austin roses, probably owned and maintained by the university. I rang the bell and the door opened and there he was. I said, 'My name is Winsome Webster. I'm your new reader.' He said, 'I'm Patrick. Come in.'

It wasn't until I was sitting in an armchair in the rather pleasant sunroom at the back that I really looked at him. I suppose he was a little younger than Oliver. Oliver's my twenty-eight-year-old son – doing a PhD in Theatre Studies at university in upstate New York. He had curly brown hair falling to his shoulders and was taller than me, and slim, but he had eyes the colour of limes and every time he looked my way I felt as if little grenades were exploding. He told me he'd always been blind. He said, 'Tell me three things about yourself' and I said, 'Well, I'm a widow. I enjoy being useful. And I can't parallel park.' He laughed. He had a lovely laugh, a ramshackle, Irish kind of a laugh, and he showed me what he wanted me to read – some rather heavy-going books about art history – and I read. I read. And every so often, he'd ask me to repeat something and I would and I'd look at him and he'd turn those unseeing eyes towards me and I couldn't quite believe anything so successfully colourful could be so unsuccessful in their purpose. I guess that's what the term 'spectacularly unsuccessful' means. They gave him a kind of intensity that was frankly off-putting. He was too big for the room. He knocked everything else out of the way. I was glad I hadn't brought scones.

I went back every Friday after that. Each time I visited, Patrick would ask me questions and I found myself telling him about my life even though there didn't seem much to

tell. I told him about Jim. I told him about the widows. I
told him about my two children. And once, when he asked
me if I enjoyed my life, I found myself saying that there
was a kind of relief in *resigning* myself to it. I didn't
struggle against it any more, and it seemed to me that life
was the long process of surviving the defeat of expectations.
What pleasures life delivers are never the expected ones. I
remembered walking to the bank one day nearly thirty years
before, in spring, with Oliver in his pram wearing my
favourite blue-and-white-striped beret and he was sitting up,
very straight and utterly lovely, smiling and happy, and I
thought to myself, I'll make poached pears tonight and I felt
this wave of utter and absolute joy that lasted just a few
moments. I have never been happier. The sun, the baby, the
pears.

   Beat.

Who would have thought that would be the highlight?

Usually, Patrick would make tea. Very deliberately and
capably, even carrying it into the sunroom on a tray, and
he'd ask me to describe the garden and I'd tell him how the
maple leaves had turned to red or how the leaves were
finally gone.

Mostly, I'd read the same kind of books: 'Those of us
who are neither collectivists believing in nations, races,
classes or periods as unified psychological entities, nor
dialectical materialists untroubled by the discovery of
"contradictions" . . .' E.H. Gombrich. No relation to Anita
Brookner. I tried to read intelligently, but at one point, I put
down the book and said, 'Patrick, I don't have the foggiest
what I'm saying.' And he said, 'Winsome, you read
magnificently.' *Winsome, you read magnificently.*

I went home and the next day I had dinner at Vonnie's –
Vonnie's done a Thai cooking class so it's all lemongrass
this and lime-leaf that, when we'd all be happier with a

chicken casserole – and I was thinking about what Patrick
had said, but I didn't say anything. And on Sunday, whilst
talking to Helen, I didn't say anything either. I was bursting
to tell a widow or two, but I felt foolish. Monday we went
to *Bridget Jones's Diary* and Tuesday we walked along the
Bluff with the labradors and Wednesday we played bridge
and Thursday we had book club and I found myself tuning
out while Allison rabbited on about V.S. Naipaul. I think
Allison believes she is the greatest living literary critic on
subcontinental fiction – it's Naipaul this and Jhabvala that –
as if the greatest living literary critic on subcontinental
fiction would spend her days in Deepdene / Croydon doing
bad oil paintings of camellias. Anyway – Friday I could
barely stand the train trip to town I was so excited. I embar-
rassed myself by the effort I was making, appearance-wise.
I'm rather a sensible-tweed-skirt-and-blouse kind of a
dresser, but I'd popped down to the boutique in the village
and picked up a black skirt and flared sort of top, which my
mother would have described contemptuously as 'exotic',
but which I considered fetching. With my silver beads, I
thought it made me look a touch bohemian, like an 'author'
or a famous feminist, or at least the kind of woman who
still had sex. Now, I know Patrick is blind, but it was really
more for me. I wanted to feel more interesting in his
company, as if I was less of a Winsome and more of an . . .
Abigail.

I sat down in the sunroom. It was a lovely day. I looked up
and in his hands was a book, no cover. 'I have something
else for you to read, Winsome.' It had a marker in it, about
a third of the way through, and I opened the page, saying,
'Of course, Patrick, whatever you like.'

Beat. She reads.

'Jefferson could see the distant figures of the women lying
by the river. It was a perfect midsummer afternoon, the
smell of honeysuckle in the air carried on a gentle breeze

and Jefferson felt the distinct sensation that the day was meant for pleasure.'

Beat.

'Jefferson felt the distinct sensation that the day was meant for pleasure.' Curious. 'When Jefferson reached the river bank, he could see –

Slowing down:

– Persephone lying . . . naked amongst the buttercups, Delia beside her in a curiously relaxed pose.' I looked up. He sat, eyes closed, his chin tilted towards the sun, as if listening intently to the words. Naked amongst the buttercups! I felt fairly sure that this was not what the Society had in mind for its readers. 'Jefferson knelt beside the hedgerows and contemplated the elegance of the female form. Delia appeared to be . . . stroking the . . . hip line of Persephone's undulating body and gazing at her with rapt intent. Softly, she ran her –

Beat.

– tongue over Persephone's rose-hued skin.' All right. All right. Enough! 'Patrick,' I cried, 'I can't read this! *I'm a widow!*' 'Keep reading, Winsome, please just keep reading.'

Reluctantly, I picked up the book again. 'Delia stood and walked down to the river and sauntered into the cool waters.' Well, thank God for that! 'Jefferson watched her swim upstream and then casually walked over to where Persephone lay. She opened her eyes and through those miraculous lashes, took in his brooding gaze.' Miraculous lashes. I mean, goodness gracious. There wasn't a single character in an Anita Brookner who had miraculous lashes, or a brooding gaze for that matter. I hadn't signed on for this and yet . . . and yet . . . It was my duty to facilitate the passage of words without passing judgement, and in all my years . . . I had never turned my back on that principle.

Well, it soon appeared that the lady in question 'had soft
yet pert breasts that erupted like vanilla bavarois from her
luscious torso, her hair in strawberry-blonde ringlets
tumbled to her waist.' I should put it on record that all my
life . . . I mean *all* my life, I have wanted hair that tumbled.

It seemed to me that Patrick had moved his body slightly in
my direction, as if leaning into the words. I summoned all
my courage. 'Jefferson undid the shiny buttons of his
military jacket and slipped it off his broad shoulders. The
top half of his body was bare, but for an impressive glade
of chest hair.' A *glade* of chest hair. 'Jefferson had started
to perspire. He turned his head down to Persephone's body
and moved his lips across her delicate skin. Softly he
danced them over her breasts and up her long neck.
Between them, Persephone felt the rock-like force of his –

   Beat.

– unstoppable –

   Beat.

– manhood.' I was feeling . . . odd. I was feeling decidedly
odd. I hadn't felt this way . . . as if tiny flames were leaping
inside of me, getting higher and higher, like the flickering of
moths inside my body as if something delicate but resilient
was waking up inside of me, was stretching and waking . . .

Suddenly, Patrick faced me and grabbed the chair I was on
and pulled it towards him, so that I was directly in front of
him. He put his hands down on my knees and slid them
simultaneously up my thighs under my new black skirt. I
thought of saying, 'Patrick!', but I could hear the potential
sound of false dismay in my voice. As I stared at those
frantically green eyes, I felt little parts of me reacting, as if
penny-bangers were going off all over my body . . . I put
the book down and shut my eyes. I felt his hands pull off
my black top which I was glad I had worn in the circum-
stances, and my . . . hug-me-tight . . . which I rather wished

I had not, and then reach around and undo my brassiere. I
stood then. I slipped off the skirt and my stockings and my
underwear. I felt the intense warmth of the autumn sun
through the glass windows. And there I was. A sixty-four-
year-old naked widow. And what were my weapons?

What did I have to rally to the situation? Wit and a clitoris!

Patrick stood, reached out for me, took hold of my elbow,
steadied himself and then ran his hands around my outline,
his fingers running the length of my torso, dipping where
I dipped, rising where I rose. He pulled off his sweater and
with his hands, drew my face to his and kissed me on the
lips, pushing into me, as if he wanted to . . . *devour* me . . .
I could feel my breasts against his . . . *glade* . . . and then
gently, gently he walked me over to the table and he swept
his hand over it – the hyacinths, the apples spilling over
onto the floor – and he pushed me gently down onto it and
he undid himself and without a word, he entered me! *Me!*
He entered *me*! And I can tell you right now, it was . . .
It was like slipping into something simultaneously familiar
and foreign, like re-entering an old dream, and yet, and
yet . . . This time, perhaps, the ecstasy – and there *was*
ecstasy – was not about possessing youth but being in touch
with it, and not out of some tedious order, the order of the
universe, of mother and son, or old lady shopper and the
young man who carries the box to the car – but out of
chance. And there is nothing more enchanting than chance –
when it goes your way.

There's a Wallace Stevens poem that uses the phrase
'pierced by a death'. I had been pierced by a death and
sweetly, sweetly, Patrick filled me up again, filled me up
with the salve of the totally unexpected.

ZOE STRUTHERS

A spotlight in the black illuminates the savagely painted
face of the ageing American diva who sings without
accompaniment:

ZOE.
I've got something to say –

The crowd erupts into wild applause.

I'm not going away –

The lights come up, the piano joins in, and the whole
woman is revealed as she continues to sing, building in
pitch and confidence, strutting her extraordinary stuff.
She walks around the edge of the stage, waving and
blowing kisses as she sings to members of the cheering
audience:

I'm not shedding a tear . . .
I'm not wearing a frown . . .
I'm not going under!
I'm not going down!

I'm not defeated at all!
I've not gone to the wall!
Say what you will and say what you do,
This baby's not met her Waterloo!

I'm turning on my engines!
I still got some thrust!
Nobody can say that I've bitten the dust . . .
My temperature's risin',
Now ain't that surprisin' –

THE LADY IS BACK!

A male show-bizzy voice.

ANNOUNCER. Ladies and gentlemen – I give you Zoe
Struthers!

*She breaks off singing to the wild applause. She takes
a moment to savour it, then beckons to the audience to
quieten down.*

ZOE. Hello, Melbourne / London!

*The crowd applauds, whistles. Bad Australian / English
accent:*

Goodonyamate! / Watchyacock!

The audience goes wild.

It is so, so, good to be back! I love this city!

You may recall that I was last on your fair shores in 1997.
A lot of water under the bridge, oh me oh my! Lot o' water.
But what doesn't kill you makes you stronger, right?

Cheers.

A lot of people – let me rephrase – a lot of the media –
doubted that I would be back. Do you have the media here?
You know, newspapers?

Pause.

You do? Right. Well, a lot of them said: 'She's over. She's
washed up.' And you know, there was a time there I would
have agreed with them.

Very serious, quiet:

For a while there, the magic vanished. I'll be honest with
you folks, I didn't really know who I was any more.

Beat.

But guess what? There was life in the old girl yet!

Cheers.

I'm here to say, that despite everything, and I mean everything, the lady is back! She's back and she's here to stay, and you hacks and cynics and nay-sayers, you had better believe it!

Wild cheers from the audience. Going mushy, tearing up, she reprises the number, the piano starting up on cue:

I've been beaten, I've been stripped,
I've been walloped and whitewashed and whipped!
They called me finished and quite diminished –

I threw a few down the hatch
When they said I'd met my match –
But –
My temperature's risin',
Now ain't that surprisin' –
The lady is back!

Wild applause from the audience.

Thank you . . . Thank you . . . You're so sweet. Did anyone ever tell you that?

Quickly consulting the note written on her palm.

Melbourne / London – I love you! And here's a little number to show you how.

She launches into a horrifically bastardised cabaret arrangement of 'Waltzing Matilda' / English medley ('Land of Hope and Glory', 'Rule Brittania', etc.)

Once a jolly swagman / Land of hope and glory . . .

Wild applause from audience.

Camped by a billabong / Mother of the free . . .

Under the shade of a coolibah tree, / Send her victorious,
Happy and glorious . . .
And he sang as he watched / Rule Britannia, Britannia
rules the waves,
And waited till his billy boiled, / Britons never never
never shall be –
You'll come a-waltzing Matilda with – / Britons never
never never shall be –

She abruptly begins another song:

Please don't applaud me,
You can't afford me –

The audience bursts into spontaneous applause.

I'm really *très chère*.
My favourite pursuit
Requires plenty of loot,
I'm a dame with charisma to spare!

Please Mister investor,
I'm silk not polyester,
I want a husband and several ex –
The shoulders I rub
Are pure country club,
My best friend's a platinum Amex!

*She breaks off to talk. The music continues to tinkle in
the background.*

You know, I believe in calling a spade a spade. I think you
all know that my husband, Darryl, left me back in '99 for
my stylist, Tiffany. It was all over CNN. That's a cable
station. Do you have cable over here?

Pause.

Right.

Then, in October, my home in Beverly Hills was razed by a
fire. The home gym, up in smoke. The guest wing – reduced

to ashes. The pool house, the hacienda, the tennis house, the indoor cinema, the six-car garage, the Japanese rock garden, the Swedish bath-house, the outdoor amphitheatre – gone!

She goes back to singing:

The thought of impecunity makes my skin crawl,
I'd rather be *nouveau* than not rich at all.
I like my Bolly,
I'm not at all prolly.
If I'm out of your reach, that's your call.

I'm croissant not crumpet,
'It girl' not strumpet,
My tastes bring a guy to his knees –
If I have an epiphany
It's always at Tiffany –
My favourite two words are: 'Charge, please!'

She breaks off again:

That same year, my mom took ill and I went to Florida to say my goodbyes and, just before she closed her eyes for the last time, she squeezed my hand and she sighed and she told me my father was not really my father. That really threw me. I'd been living a lie! I had to grapple with some tough issues, I had to relocate my self-belief. I had to learn not to hide from the question: 'Who *is* Zoe Struthers?'

Sings:

I'd never stop ya
Taking me to the opera,
I like culture within certain reason.
Believe me, I'll shout
When I'm all Wagnered out,
I'm Gucci or Pucci all season.

She goes back to talking:

And then in November, the baby girl I had once given away at birth came back to me – a beautiful nineteen-year-old.

Her name is Deirdre and she is the love of my life . . . Even
if she doesn't feel the same way. There's a lot of anger.
There's a lot of rage. And that's good. That's a good thing.
And one day, one day, I hope that Deirdre will find it in her
heart to stop saying those things to *Entertainment Weekly*
about me and learn to accept me for who I am instead of
who I was, just as I will accept her for who she is instead of
who I want her to be . . .

Sings:

Well, goodness me,
Not Beluga for tea,
So bring on the Dom Perignon –

Please don't applaud me,
You can't afford me,
I'm really *très chère*.
My favourite pursuit
Requires plenty of loot,
I'm a dame with charisma to spare . . .

Applause.

A lot of change. A lot of give. A lot of take. A lot of
learning. A lot of pain. I tried to find solace in the bottle.
I tried to hide from life. I gave in to the demons. Have you
heard of substance abuse over here?

Pause.

You have? Right. So when Deirdre found me I realised that
I owed a lot of people. I owed her. I owed you. I owed
Mastercard. And I owed myself. So I said, I said, 'Zoe,
you can crawl into the gutter and give up or you can look
yourself square in the eye and stop feeling sorry for
yourself.' So I fought. Man, how hard I fought those little
demons. And I must have had some help from somebody
up there –

Indicating heaven.

– because as I stand here before you –

Tottering:

– *I Am Sober.*

Applause from the audience.

And here's a little number to show you what I've learned:

Sings:

> If you're in a travelling mood,
> Baby, I don't want to be rude,
> But I'll say it once and again –
> Here's my very best thought,
> Don't get yourself a passport
> To the terrible country of men.

> If you travel the world, it's plain to tell
> The original caveman is alive and well.
> Wherever you mingle,
> He's quite multilingual
> And ready to do the hard-sell!

> In New York, every dude
> Can be awfully crude,
> Put your sexual charms in their cage.
> In LA, every heel
> Wants a three-picture deal!
> The Isle of Wight can turn a girl beige.

> And if the urge ever seizes ya
> When you're in Indonesia,
> Make sure that you stick to the rules.
> In Japan, they're pushy
> For more than their sushi,
> So keep your wasabi quite cool!

If you travel the world, it's plain to tell
The original caveman is alive and well.
Wherever you mingle,
He's quite multilingual
And ready to do the hard-sell!

Let's scat –

Scat and dance break.

Get out of there pronto
If you're in Toronto,
There's too much to lose in Toulouse.
If in Peking you're stuck,
Enjoy a good (*beat*) duck –
Don't vamp your way down to Vaduz.

Like it or not,
In Chile they're hot!
And unless your head's full of holes,
Here's the last of my tips,
Take the time, read my lips,
Stay away from both of the Poles!

If you're in a travelling mood,
Baby, I don't want to be rude,
But I'll say it once and again –
Here's my very best thought,
Don't get a passport
To the terrible country of men!

Wild applause.

Goodnight, Melbourne / London!